A CENTURY OF DAILY RECORD LAUGHS

A CENTURY OF DAILY RECORD LAUGHS

compiled by
ROD McLEOD

MAINSTREAM
PUBLISHING

First published in Great Britain in 1994
by Mainstream Publishing Company (Edinburgh) Ltd
7 Albany Street, Edinburgh EH1 3UG

ISBN 1 85158 667 9

The proceeds of this book are being
donated to the **Children's Hospice Appeal, Scotland**

————————

Printed in Great Britain by Scotprint Ltd, Musselburgh

ROD McLEOD is the latest in a long line
of artists to grace the *Daily Record's* pages with his cartoons.
In this book, he casts his eye over the *Daily Record's*
drawings and cartoons since 1895 and chooses
the best of them to celebrate the paper's
centenary in 1995.

CONTENTS

The cavemen were pretty good at them. Though chiselling out a cartoon meant these early examples weren't able to meet a Daily Record deadline. The Egyptians knew a thing or two about using drawings to trace the progress of society as well. And the much revered Old Masters who painted some of the world's great art treasures were also capable of drawing their subject in something almost qualifying as caricature. But it wasn't until the 1600s that such drawings were actually used as a means of ridicule. Over the centuries since, the cartoon has matured and developed into many different forms. Often those which became the subject of most comment were drawn at periods of great upheaval.

The French Revolution and two World Wars have all been fertile territory for those cartoonists who specialised in politics and current events. The best of them live on long after their creators have departed to the great studio in the sky. People still remember the classic caricature, by the wartime and post war cartoonist Vicky, of premier Harold Macmillan in which he dressed him up as 'Supermac'. Later there was the cartoon created by Jak at the time of the Six Days War in the Middle East. 'Come to Israel and See the Pyramids' was his ironic caption, under a drawing of the major Egyptian tourist attraction! Images like that underline just what a powerful medium cartoons can be, not just in relfecting the imagination of the artists, but reflecting the ideas and opinions of the times. For that very reason, they also became propaganda weapons in states like Stalin's

Russia or Hitler's Germany where it was quite literally more than the cartoonist's life was worth to send up the government of the day. Instead, the government would use their pen and wit to send a particular set of signals to the general public. Some people have called cartoons the slang of graphic art, but that almost does them less than justice. Cartoons are often wickedly funny, but at times of tragedy, such as famine, they can also emerge as a poignant and devestating portrait of reality, And, like photographs, can be more powerful and dramatic than the words of the writer which they illustrate.

Most cartoonists would agree that the art of caricature is almost a separate skill. Many very amusing cartoonists have never acquired the difficult knack of portraying a well-known face in such a fashion as to make them instantly recognisable, while using enough exaggeration to add wit and style to the portrait.

Conversely, some of the finest draughtsmen and women in the world have never had any particular facility with jokes!

There is a general belief that the people who make us laugh in our newspapers and magazines through their artwork must be extremely amusing in real life. Not so. It's well known that some of the funniest artists are positively morose around the house .. . ask their spouses!

Very few of the top names would regard themselves as comedians who happen to be able to draw. In fact, in order to find a ready joke in a topical situation you have to have a very particular mindset . . . one which will often let you tie up two apparently unrelated news events,

After the caricature and the topical cartoon came the immense popularity of comic strips, the best of which are laughed at in syndication round the world. Proof positive that there are at least some things the whole world finds funny . Go into any office in the world and you're liable to see a strip of Peanuts, or Andy Capp, or Hagar pinned up. Perhaps because they rely on human weakness and frailty for their subject matter, and there's no shortage of these commodities wherever you look.

Comic strips in essence have become the newspaper soap operas of our time. Readers who got caught up in the West Highland shenanigans of Angus Og would want their daily fix in much the same way that horoscope addicts turn first to that part of the paper.

Over all these cartoon forms, Scotland has had its share of incomparable talents. Bud Neill's gallus Glaswegians became national institutions and went on to become the subject of television documentaries and successful books.

In fact, Bud's immortal Wild West characters, who all, naturally, spoke fluent Glaswegian, even have a statue built in their honour by public subscription. Now, that's staying power.

But it's not just fans who find cartoons so fascinating. For historians they provide a priceless glimpse into different decades, different generations, and different social styles. They tell us a great deal about the life and times in which the artist worked and, just as valuably, about the spirit of the audience. Living would be a much duller business without them.

A CENTURY OF LAUGHS

In the Early Days... well, around the twenties

October 1895, and the *Daily Record* first appeared on the streets of Scotland; a paper without cartoons.

In fact the pages of the new 'Voice of Scotland' looked more like a broadsheet than a tabloid. Early front pages were a mixture of news and adverts; international news jostled with reports from local burgh

" Robbed " Roy: It's high time ye put a stop to this, or maybe we'll hae a hangin' match.
Bailie Nicol Jarvie: Ah-eh-oh! Ma conscience! Hang a Bailie?

THE THREE-LEGGED RACE.

Fritz:– Stick it, Hans!   United we stand, divided they fall!

courts, councils and churches. The motor-car wasn't yet with us so the adverts were mostly for coachmen and grooms. Royal news was pretty scurrilous, revealing what Queen Victoria had for lunch.

Fashion drawings in adverts appeared in the early years but it took time for the illustrators of the day to realise that the newspaper was a natural outlet; somewhere they could express their opinions and exert influence.

The first regular cartoons in the *Daily Record* started

appearing around the 1920s. They were highly realistic and, not surprisingly, they commented on the hot topics of the day. Eustace and Ivanhoe were two artists who pioneered political cartooning in the *Record*, with wonderful

THE MUD-SLINGERS.

John Bull:—" I don't mind you boys slinging mud at each other, but what about my good name-plate?"

The French-Asquith-Smith-Dorrien controversy, according to foreign reports, is simply bringing the good name of Great Britain into disrepute.

THE DANGEROUS "RATE" OF EDUCATION.

"IVANHOE" '9.

[With apologies to Harry Tate.
The Passenger: But isn't this a fearful rate?   The Driver: Not at all.   We'll soon make it higher still.   The Passenger: But you'll get run in!   The Driver: No, but that chap looks like getting run over.—This striking cartoon is reproduced from the "Sunday Mail."

line drawings and witty, if somewhat lengthy, captions.

Jumble and Oddment Sales were often the front page leads in those days. But the first Labour government in 1924 found news stories taking over the front pages and thus the birth of new opportunities for the illustrator/cartoonist. Of course, it's always easier for the cartoonist, when the readers know the story before reading the cartoon. So page one news stories proved a real bonus.

RODGER

FILM   FAVOURITES. — William Powell as Rodger sees him.

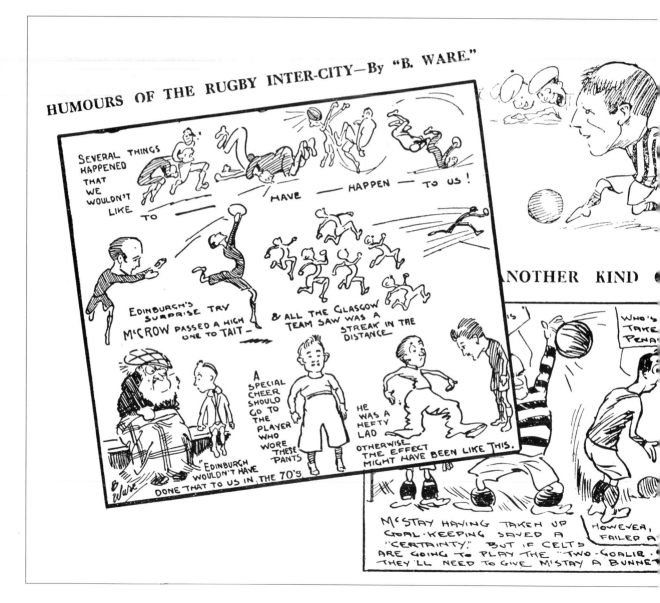

HUMOURS OF THE RUGBY INTER-CITY—By "B. WARE."

While news cartoons gradually emerged in what was normally a 12-page paper, the first sporting cartoons also began to appear. The now traditional Monday morning post-mortem after the Saturday afternoon game began in the *Record*. Under the pen name of 'B Ware', the artist gave an illustrated and amusing round-up of football and rugby to the readers. Individual caricatures were part of the staple diet of both sporting and topical cartoonists at this time.

It's safe to say that these less than flattering cartoon portraits were appreciated more by the readers than the subjects involved!

LIPSE BY GALLAGHER AND SONS.—BY "B. WARE."

Enter… Pip, Squeak and Wilfred

The *Daily Record*, now firmly established and costing just one penny (a price it was to keep for 20 years), was now in tabloid mode – strong bold pages fighting for Scottish issues. But it never forgot its other duty to entertain its readers. With the number of pages on the increase, the *Record* could devote space to more laughs.

Pip, Squeak and Wilfred, a syndicated cartoon strip (it also appeared in other newspapers), began its run. It featured a dog, a penguin and a rabbit, and although the storylines were sometimes very involved they were always entertaining and sometimes even educational!

MY PETS SEE THEMSELVES AT A XMAS BAZAAR.

1. "A parcel for you, Squeak," said Postie.

2. "I wonder what it is?" cried Squeak.

3. Then out popped two sweet little ducklings.

4. Delighted, the pets brought them water.

1. Pip and Squeak entered for the sack race—

2. —at the village sports. Squeak was very nervous.

3. When a pistol was fired to start the race—

4. —she immediately thought she had been shot!

5. After the race (won by Pip), Squeak—

6. —was surprised to find that she wasn't wounded!

Bringing Up Father...

Another syndicated strip which started around this time was 'Bringing Up Father'. Distributed by the International Feature Service in America, this beautifully drawn and very popular cartoon featured for almost 30 years in the *Record*. Not really so surprising, because although it was American through and through, its main theme was the battlefield inhabited by husband and wife. Always a winning combination.

The *Daily Record* was by now well established in virtually every household in the land and the cartoon had become a permanent feature in its pages – the topical campaigning illustration on the news or foreign pages, the strips throughout the features pages and the occasional sports commentary at the back.

The cartoon, whether illuminating the main story, appealing to the the common domestic sense of humour, or capturing the essence of the main sporting story of the day, had become an art form in its own right; a part of that indefinable but important package which attracts and keeps reader loyalty.

We're Now Approaching the Thirties... and the pace is hotting-up

The thirties certainly offered the topical cartoon illustrator plenty of scope. Income tax, national service, international propaganda, war and peace, gave cartoonists Cecil Orr, Rodger and Dzke White loads of subject matter for their pen. All three featured with their up-to-the-minute satirical drawings throughout that troubled decade and beyond.

Germany's Dark Horse.

The famous Government-owned Tumbrel isn't the only horse that wins races for them.

On His Own Hook.

The Horrors of the " Third Degree."

Another Art Sensation In The Offing.

Making It Snappy

National Government propaganda by mobile cinema begins to-day.
Our cartoonist suggests a few special features.

Income tax return forms are now being sent out.

Looking for sporting comments and illustrations at this time, the *Record* found someone on its own doorstep. Jack Lindsay worked in the print production department but was also a talented artist and cartoonist. Lindsay, his pen name, majored in football in the Monday morning slot. His speciality was humorous drawings and well observed comments on our national game. And even in those days, the exploits of those warriors who donned the battle dress of the Scottish strip were a rich source of material for artists who didn't lack a sense of humour. It's worth reflecting that if our national team had ever been in serious danger of winning a world cup, generations of cartoonists would have been out of business!

Enter... Lauder, Willis and Gordon

The *Record* was always looking for new ideas to enhance its pages and entertain it's readers. The 'Lauder, Willis and Gordon' cartoon strip certainly did that. What did the trick was the fact that it was very Scottish, featured Scots folk and mentioned well-known Scottish places.

This has long proved a selling point for those newspapers who have cultivated their core audience. It is no accident that the *Daily Record* adopted a slogan of being edited, printed and published in Scotland. Patriotism sells papers.

and Donald Duck

Of course, intrinsically Scottish cartoon strips were few and far between. But as the entertainment content of the paper increased, so too did the efforts of the *Record* to showcase the best available. And they didn't come any bigger than straight from the pen of Walt Disney Studios. Which brings us to the acquisition of Donald Duck. Donald and friends were to feature in the paper throughout most of the thirties and forties.

And while we're speaking about the fabulous forties . . .

The Difficult Years

The war, which brought in its wake both immense courage and unimaginable horrors, tested to the full the comic talents of the illustrators and cartoonists of that era. There is nothing very amusing about conflict, yet there is arguably no more important moment in which to raise the spirits of a nation and remind it of the the power of humour to replenish the human soul.

Of necessity the *Daily Record* was reduced in size. There were fewer pages, fewer adverts, fewer pictures, fewer illustrations and, inevitably, fewer cartoons. But those available to draw for newspapers during this time did a wonderful job in keeping the nation smiling. Their contribution to the national morale should not be underestimated. Often some of the jokes which circulated in the darker moments of the war years were cut out and sent to serving soldiers, sailors and airmen, and staple fare like Mac and Harry Smith became, in their way, an important part of Britain's war effort.

MAC

NIPPON YUSEN KAISAH TROUBLE
" GET IT, NAZIS? THEY'RE PUTTIN' THE NIP ON YOUSE IN CASE A' TROUBLE ! "

MAC

IT'S A FAR,FAR "BUTTER" THING
RATIONING WON'T HURT US HAM ACTORS WE'LL DO SHAKESPEARE AND SAVE OUR BACON

MAC

THE TRAIL OF THE LONESOME PINT
" US STOUT FELLERS LIKE WORKING IN SCOTLAND, WHERE EVERY LUMBERJACK CAN FIND A GILL ! "

HARRY SMITH

Much the same could be said of the 'Breakfast Smile' which, unusually, was the product of several different pens. But despite a variety of authors the smiles could always be relied upon to capture the popular mood of the moment. This was a war being waged on several different fronts, and the cartoonists were an important component in stoking the home fires, whilst giving long distance support to the men and women serving at the sharp end. Laughter can't end conflict, but sometimes it makes it more bearable.

" Watch your tank, M'sieu? "

BREAKFAST SMILE

" Now we just saunter up and ask the time, it always averts suspicion."

" Pardon me, sir, but you don't half 'spill the beans in your sleep, sir."

" A ha'penny! Another of those tip and run eaters!"

*" Omelette for four hundred—
get cracking!"*

Football too continued to play its part and Jack Lindsay returned to his regular Monday morning commentry on the weekend sport, as illustrated on the following pages.

It took some time after the war years for the paper to increase its pagination and some time also for old and new cartoonists to emerge. But emerge they did...

*" I know sir — and I've
reported it to the laundry,
sir."*

*" That is the end of the
news . . . here are the head-
lines again!"*

HAVING BEEN TOLD IN OUR YOUTH THAT IT WAS ONLY "WEE COOPERS WHA LEEVED IN FIFE, NICKETTY, NACKETTY, BLAH, BLAH, BLAH!" ——

NAE WEE COOPERS, ONY A BIG AITKEN PAIN!

RANGERS V. EAST FIFE

THE MINER'S DREAM OF HOME

WE WERE INTERESTED TO HEAR THAT EAST FIFE HAD QUITE A FEW MINERS IN THEIR TEAM, SO LEAVING "WAVERLEY" TO TELL YOU HOW THEY PLAY FOOTBALL WE WILL

CONCENTRATE ON TELLING YOU HOW THEY TRAIN FOR IT. REAL TOUGH BABIES THESE MINERS, THEY DON'T HACK OUT COAL WITH ANYTHING SO EFFEMINATE AS A PICK, THEY KICK IT TO BITS WITH THEIR FITBA' BOOTS.

WHICH PRODUCES GUYS LIKE SAMMY STEWART WHOSE TRAINING CONSISTS OF A LITTLE LIGHT MASSAGE WITH A SHOVEL AND WHO THINKS NOTHING OF A 'STINT' THE SIZE OF WILLIE WADDELL.

THEN THERE'S JIMMY PHILP WHO HAD TO HAVE A HUGE PATCH ON HIS EYE. IF MR. PHILP'S HEAD HAD COME RIGHT OFF IN A TACKLE

BEND DOON TILL AH PLASTER YE!

AH'LL KEEP THE HEID, YOU DON'T NEED TAE!

HIS TRAINER WOULD HAVE STUCK PLASTER ON HIS NECK AND TOLD HIM NO' TAE BE A BIG SAFTIE.

DEFINITELY A HARD BUNCH, THESE FIFERS, RANGERS ARE VERY GLAD THERE ISN'T A WEST, NORTH OR SOUTH FIFE,

DUNCAN, A REAL HAZEL NUT.

WHIT'S IN A NAME, THEY'RE A' TOUGH!

JACK LINDSAY

AT WHICH HIBS GIVE A HOLLOW LAUGH AND MUTTER IN A-MAYES-MENT, "HAVEN'T YOU EVER HEARD OF DUNFERMLINE?

Without Words

Into the Fifties... and there's nothing like an election to bring out the cartoonists

Whenever the cartoonist is sitting staring at that blank sheet of paper, scrabbling for inspiration, desperately searching for a new idea, the one event which saves his bacon is... another election. And the Fifties were kind enough to bring a whole batch of them.

VOTE LABOUR

NOT TOO LITTLE —

VOTE LIBERAL

— NOT TOO MUCH —

VOTE CONSERVATIVE

— BUT JUST RIGHT !!

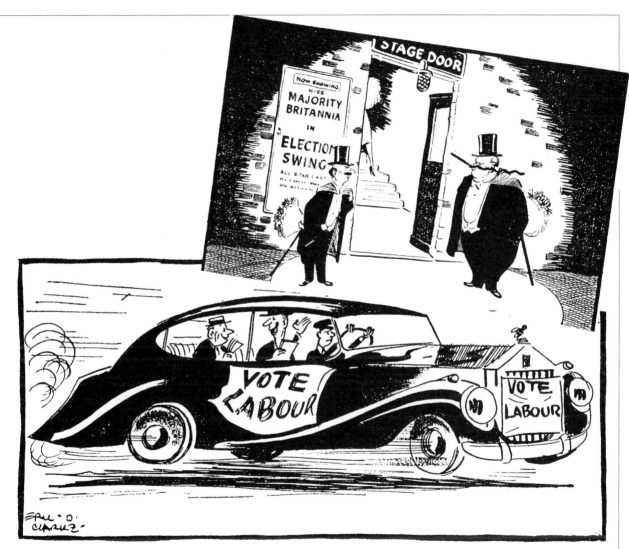

"Then you come to the bit about fair shares and bloated capitalists!"

or a Budget

And no matter who gets in, the new government will assure the electorate that they are in a mess because the last lot couldn't count. In contrast they are now about to bring in a really sensible budget. And what they all forget is that voters hate taxes whoever thinks them up.

MAC says: "*We'll be making some nice election custard pies!*"

MAC says: "*Wales is having a Covenant, too. It agrees that London can't govern*

The fifties also brought a fresh outbreak of tabloid wars . . . and an urgent need to deploy some fresh troops. The *Record* recruited a couple of crackers! On the home front the wit and wisdom of the incomparable Mac was deployed alongside the international nitwittery of Useless Eustace, whose popularity with women readers might well have had something to do with the fact that he confirmed all their suspicions about the brain power of the average man! But for whatever reason, Mac and Eustace became a dynamic duo who kept the *Record's* reputation for spotting cartoon winners intact.

MAC says: "*Ach, oor right wing's ower conservative, and oor left's labourin' a bit.*"

MAC says: "*And here is a final report on the Budget—*"

MAC says: "*No, the census won't get you a house, but it'll put you in a nice pigeonhole.*"

MAC says: "*The Grand National makes my heart jump—thirty times, twice round the course.*"

A CENTURY OF LAUGHS

" You and your darned candlelight dinners! "

" You'll find your pay packet a little heavier in future, Fishwick— We're using thicker envelopes!!"

"Things are getting me down, Doc. — can you stiffen my upper lip?!"

" A fine time you picked to play see-saw, I must say ! "

Og, Capp and Neill...
a hat-trick of goodies

If Mac and Eustace were a timely twosome, Angus Og, Andy Capp and Bud Neill were certainly a midfield trio to conjure with. Almost an embarrassment of riches for the editor of the day, but all different enough to command their own loyal army of fans. First to sign up was Bud Neill, an enigmatic figure in real life, but a legend to those who lapped up his wee Glesca wifies and the incomparable Lobey Dosser.

Bud's first cartoon in the Record

" Nae eatin' chits in the caur, you. Ye wantin' mice aboot the place ?"

"Pay nae attention, son. It's jist yir Granpa limberin' up for Hogmanay . . ."

* "Could ye come back the morn aboot nine an' we'll make a day o' it?" *

"Deid romantical. It all sterted when he drapped a pokey hat doon her blouse."

BUD NEILL

" Naebody's goin' tae spill Mrs. Thomson ower tae Wick, are they, Mrs. Thomson? "

HAPPY DAYS TO ALL READERS IN 1958...

" This is the night faither goes an' frightens the life oot his ulcer...."

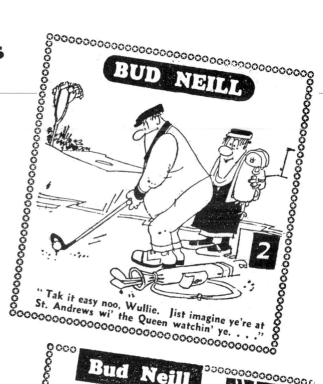

BUD NEILL

" Tak it easy noo, Wullie. Jist imagine ye're at St. Andrews wi' the Queen watchin' ye...."

Bud Neill

" Ye can stop lookin' for the budgie... "

"That reminds me, I've nothin' for me man's tea ..."

"D'ye no' think the Saltcoats polis'll be busy enough in July?"

"Disnae hauf fancy his barra, tae. Calls himsel' a black - an' - white artist ..."

And, in addition to these household characters, the strips pages were adding to their cast list with more syndicated offerings like The Flutters. Albert and Bert might seem a pretty inept breed of wide-boys to today's audience, but in their time they were the likely lads that everyone turned to. If Arthur Daley had begun his career in dodgy deals in newspapers, he'd probably have made his debut in this slot.

But as would be con men, this pair couldn't hold a candle to the man who provided the original design format for Britain's best-known male chauvinist pig. Reg Smythe couldn't have known that he'd given birth to a legend when he created Andy Capp.

THE FLUTTERS
Albert and Bert

THE FLUTTERS
Albert and Bert

Reg had actually been drawing for the *Record*'s sister paper, the *Mirror*, for some time before Andy and all his works were unleashed on the Scottish public. And he certainly revised their opinion of how the average English gent might behave. Andy's missus, the long suffering Florrie, did of course

' I can't bear to see a woman standing "

" Don't make the holiday arrangements myself—my wife tells me where, my boss tells me when, and my bank manager tells me how long."

have Andy's number. But that didn't always keep her ahead on points as the husband who gave boorishness a bad name continued his rake's progress around the clubs, pubs and snooker halls of the north of England. Scottish wives weren't exactly unfamiliar with the breed. They just didn't fancy Andy giving their spouses more bad ideas.

"If it comes to that, YOU don't look so pretty in the morning either!"

"If there's one thing gets me down it's gettin' up!"

" I think I'll make me way back to the chara, Florrie—the sight
of all this water makes me feel sick! "

By the time the sixties came along the Laugh! page was also in full swing. This was the spot which showcased the pocket cartoon, offering scope to all kinds of new talent who flooded the *Record* office with their ideas. But what made them different from the modern breed was the fact that they went for a timeless gag rather than gearing their humour to the hot topic of the day. Alongside the Laugh! page in pocket form ran Calamity Gulch, a Wild Western belle who gave as good as she got! Top names like Keith Waite, the *Daily Mirror* political cartoonist also featured around the time.

"... and now, ladies and gentlemen—Marvo, and his blasted performing dogs!"

"Reelot Underfloor Heating?—I wish to make a complaint."

"This is the very LAST time Ah help you guys out wi' a flag o' truce!"

"It was a flight of three hundred storks that brought you—now shut up!"

Laugh!

"The Prime Minister has assured us that there is no cause for alarm."

"I'd keep out of his Majesty's way this morning—there's been another big oil strike in the North Sea."

"Well, it's not necessarily going to be abolished in THIS house."

Into the Sixties with the Adventures of Angus Og

Angus Og had a close shave with destiny before he found his true home in the *Record*. He'd been born in *The Bulletin*, a mainly picture paper which was about to fall victim to the market forces of the day. But on the 1st of July 1960 the *Record* threw him a lifeline and he 'chust neffer' looked back.

Drawn by art teacher Ewen Bain the wily Angus, native Utter Hebridean, roamed the parish of Drambeg with his soul mate Lachie Mohr, intent on doing as little work as possible and, at all costs, avoiding the lovelorn Mairleen.

ANGUS OG

ANGUS OG

more Angus Og later… and in colour

ANGUS OG

ANGUS OG

Through the Sixties and into the Seventies

This was to prove a golden period for the *Record* as it began to overhaul, and finally overtake, the sales totals of all its rivals. And, again, part of the winning package was a cartoon element which soon became a page. Angus retained his pole position at the top, but plumbed into the mix, widening the appeal, came more sure-fire winners from syndicated stables including the ever popular Perishers. In some ways this resembled a UK version of Peanuts in as much as it starred some quarrelsome kids orchestrated by a female mini-mobster, all ultimately outgunned by a lovable, daffy dog.

THE PERISHERS

DRAWN BY DENNIS COLLINS • WRITTEN BY MAURICE DODD

THE PERISHERS

This was the era in which the *Record* pioneered daily colour which made the next move, colour cartoons, inevitable. Many of these were imported from the other side of the Atlantic. Vivienne Green brought us both 'Kisses' and 'Love Is'. That in turn spawned 'Agony Is'... and subsequently 'Aphrodite' and 'Virginia' by the artist Leon. They became fashionable around the hey day of the Page Three girls and left about the same time. They might have been funny, but we were moving into rather more politically correct times.

AGONY IS...

... realising you've missed opening time.

AGONY IS...

... wondering where the disc jockeys get their jokes from.

AGONY IS...

... realising mother-in-law isn't staying for a short weekend.

AGONY IS...

... when she serves curry on hot days.

"So — I'm talking to myself. So what?"

A CENTURY OF LAUGHS

'Sammy' by Roger Mahoney, a cartoon about small ground-level creatures, and 'Small World' by the well-respected Don Roberts, a strip about small ground-level humans, plus 'Roz', mainly about a thinking cat created by Peter Plant, also featured in the pioneering colour cartoon section, proudly dubbed the *only* colour cartoon page in a British daily newspaper. And so it was for some time to come... These offerings were to set the standard along with the other regular *Daily Record* favourites. And they laid the groundwork for a cartoon section in the *Daily Record* which is still the UK market leader.

The LAUGH PARADE

"Oh, Wallace lives his life, and I live mine."

"Congratulations, Capitan, you've been mentioned in dispatches—you're to be shot!"

POLICE BALL

"Aren't you from traffic control?"

"My slippers are facing the wrong way."

"Don't be silly— we're not important enough to have a motorcycle escort!"

" one shepherd's pie -- and hurry ! "

From the Seventies through to the Nineties

While the Laughs! continued in colour and black and white another name joined the paper...

 a cartoonist of the pocket sized variety, hailed from the orient – arriving via the *West Lothian Courier* and the *Edinburgh Evening News*.

Surviving the initial culture shock, Rod launched into the daily adventure of trying to keep up with the sporting ongoings of the SFA, Rangers, the SFA, Celtic, the SFA, Hearts and Hibs, the SFA, the SRU, the SLTA, the SFL, the... well, all other sports organisations starting with 's'.

Rod, still stubbornly in black and white, now also contributes a topical news cartoon, thus proving that sports fans can do joined-up thinking as well. And when you think about it, politicians, soccer managers, civil servants, tennis stars, princesses, captains of industry and fly halfs all have much the same capacity to make a mess of their chosen trade. And there's just nothing more useful to the jobbing daily cartoonist than folks managing to get things spectacularly wrong.

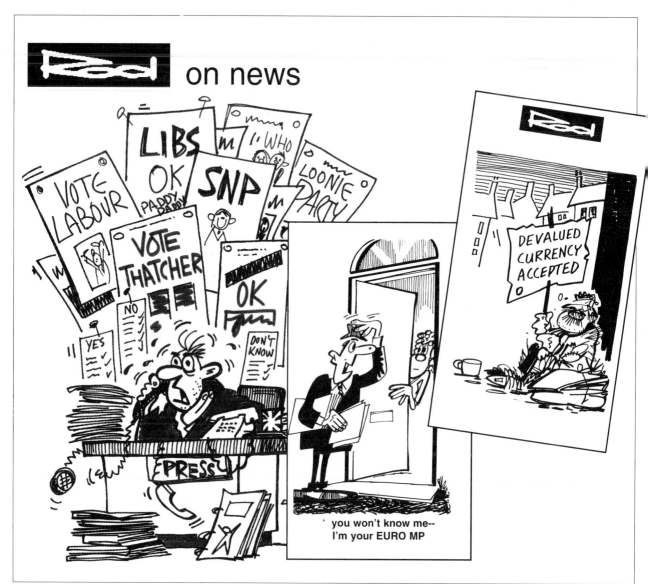

' you won't know me--
I'm your EURO MP

DEVALUED CURRENCY ACCEPTED

' IS HE A LLOYDS NAME... '

' ofcourse --- its only
an ESTIMATED reading... '

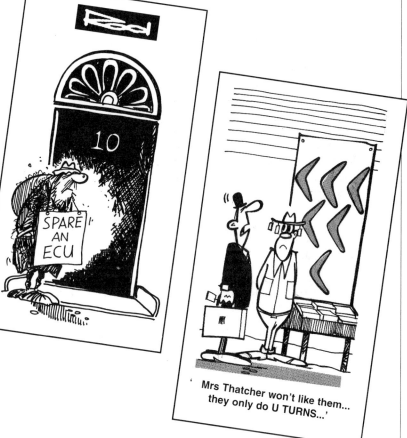

' Mrs Thatcher won't like them...
they only do U TURNS...'

' How humiliating ---
I surrendered to
KATE ADIE...'

' AM I IN THE
RIGHT PLACE...'

' Here they come...CBS, ABC,
NBC, BBC, SKY, ITN, ZDF.
DSF and CNN ... '

' I'm not happy doctor ---
I may take my illness
elsewhare... '

' FOLLOW WHAT USED TO
BE THE RAIN FORREST..'

' YOU'VE BEEN AT THE
BEACH AGAIN... '

' I honestely don't know
how many a day ---
I'm a passive smoker ... '

' SHE LOOKS MORE LIKE
A PRIME MINISTER THAN
A QUEEN...'

on SPORT...

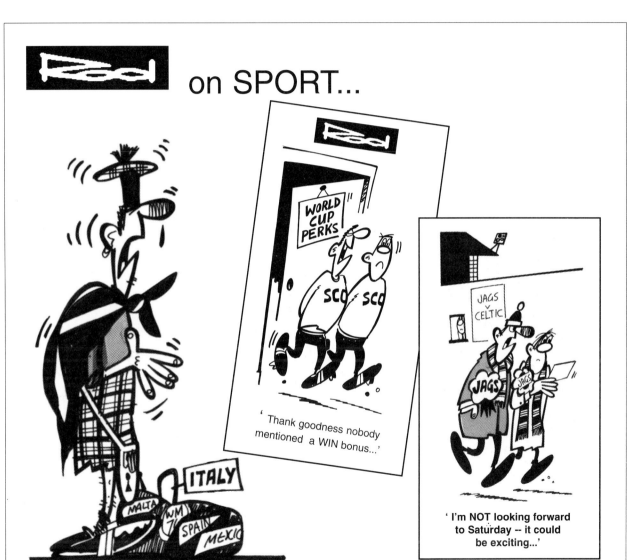

' Thank goodness nobody mentioned a WIN bonus...'

' I'm NOT looking forward to Saturday -- it could be exciting...'

' YOUR BALL IS SAFE
MONTY...'

' WE'VE HAD A LATE ENTRY --
DAVID WILKIE... '

' If I play as badly again --
I'm going to fire you...'

A CENTURY OF LAUGHS

' Just think -- in 20 years he'll be able to play for the under 16 team... '

' ... DISAPPOINTED --- I EVEN FORGOT TO MUG SOMEBODY... '

' But ref - what evidence do you have...'

' Wullie - we could win
the World Cup...'

' CAN I BORROW THE
SHEET AFTER YOU...'

" ITS GOIN' TO THE
HALL OF FAME..."

' DON'T WORRY, YOU'LL GET
USED TO IT...'

But let's return to that Hebridean hooligan, Angus Og, unofficial laird of Drambeg...

ANGUS OG

Angus, it was, who first made that bold step into glorious technicolour!

So now enjoy an early Angus Og adventure, with the bonus of today's colour stalwarts ... 'Shuggie and Duggie', Tom Bullimore and Kev White's adventures over a wall; 'Prince of the Palace' by Michael Atkinson – corgi tales from inside Buck House; Bryan Walker's 'Grandad and the Lad', the problems of a grandad with a grand lad; and 'A Man Called Horace' from Andrew Christine and Roger Kettle featuring a bear, a snake, and other assorted animals including cowboys and indians.

Proof, if any were needed, that every age produces men and women able to make us laugh at ourselves. Who knows where the cartoonists of the next century will come from? The only safe bet is that if they're good enough, and funny enough, you'll find them in the pages of the *Daily Record*.

LOOKING FOR ANGUS?

He's in our new colour cartoon section on Page 37

A MAN CALLED HORACE by ANDREW CHRISTINE and ROGER KETTLE

GRANDAD and the LAD — by BRYAN WALKER

TYPICAL! MILES FROM HOME AND IT HAS TO RAIN!

IT'S ONLY A SHOWER GRANDAD

BRUU 1177 A

I PUT THIS HAT ON TO KEEP THE *SUN* OFF MY HEAD!!

WELL.. IT SEEMS TO BE WORKING

SHUGGIE and DUGGIE — by TOM BULLIMORE and KEV WHITE